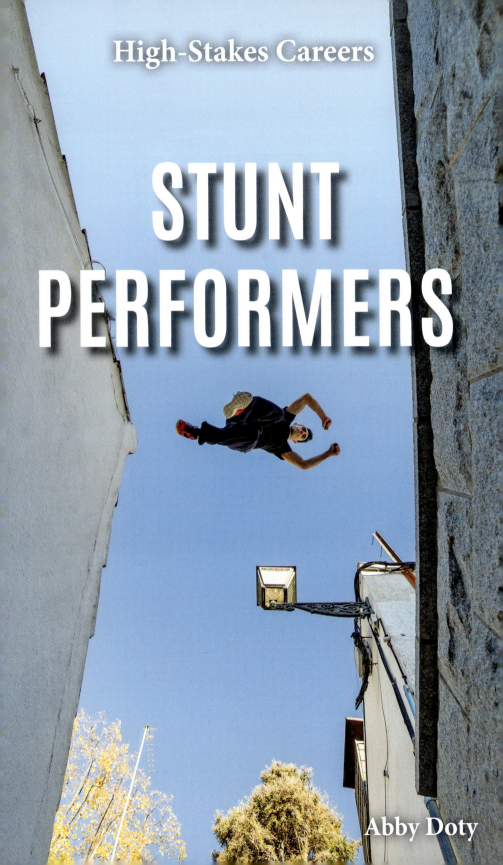

WWW.APEXEDITIONS.COM

Copyright © 2026 by Apex Editions, Mendota Heights, MN 55120. All rights reserved. No part of this book may be reproduced or utilized in any form or by any means without written permission from the publisher.

Apex is distributed by North Star Editions:
sales@northstareditions.com | 888-417-0195

Produced for Apex by Red Line Editorial.

Photographs ©: iStockphoto, cover, 1, 18–19; TCD/Prod.DB/Alamy, 4–5; Liliane Lathan/Getty Images Entertainment/Getty Images, 6–7; Shutterstock Images, 8–9, 10–11, 12–13, 14–15, 20–21, 28–29, 30–31, 32–33, 34–35, 36–37, 40–41, 42–43, 46–47, 50–51, 52–53, 54–55, 56–57, 58; Gabe Ginsberg/Getty Images Entertainment/Getty Images, 16–17; Hulton Archive/Getty Images, 22–23; Patrick Pleul/picture-alliance/dpa/AP Images, 24–25; Mark Mainz/Getty Images Entertainment/Getty Images, 26–27; Bettmann/Getty Images, 39; Thanh V. Tran/AP Images, 44–45; Stephen Chung/EMPICS/Alamy Live News/Alamy, 49

**Library of Congress Control Number: 2025930920**

**ISBN**
979-8-89250-673-1 (hardcover)
979-8-89250-707-3 (ebook pdf)
979-8-89250-691-5 (hosted ebook)

Printed in the United States of America
Mankato, MN
082025

## NOTE TO PARENTS AND EDUCATORS

Apex books are designed to build literacy skills in striving readers. Exciting, high-interest content attracts and holds readers' attention. The text is carefully leveled to allow students to achieve success quickly.

# TABLE OF CONTENTS

Chapter 1
## FANCY FALL  4

Chapter 2
## KINDS OF STUNTS  8

Chapter 3
## STUNTS ON SET  18

Chapter 4
## LIVE STUNTS  28

Story Spotlight
## EVEL KNIEVEL  38

Chapter 5
## BIG RISKS  40

Story Spotlight
## DAVID HOLMES  48

Chapter 6
## TYPES OF TRAINING  51

SKILLS CHECKLIST • 59
COMPREHENSION QUESTIONS • 60
GLOSSARY • 62
TO LEARN MORE • 63
ABOUT THE AUTHOR • 63
INDEX • 64

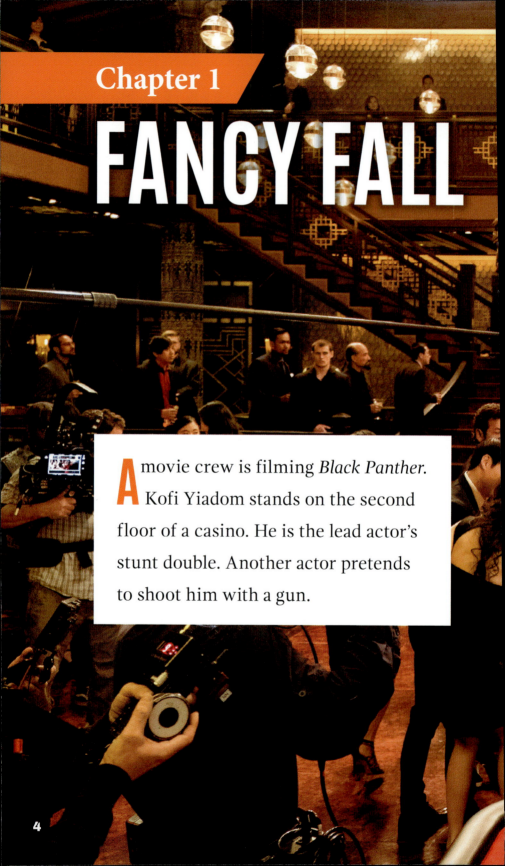

## Chapter 1
# FANCY FALL

A movie crew is filming *Black Panther*. Kofi Yiadom stands on the second floor of a casino. He is the lead actor's stunt double. Another actor pretends to shoot him with a gun.

The crew of *Black Panther* created a casino set to film a fight scene.

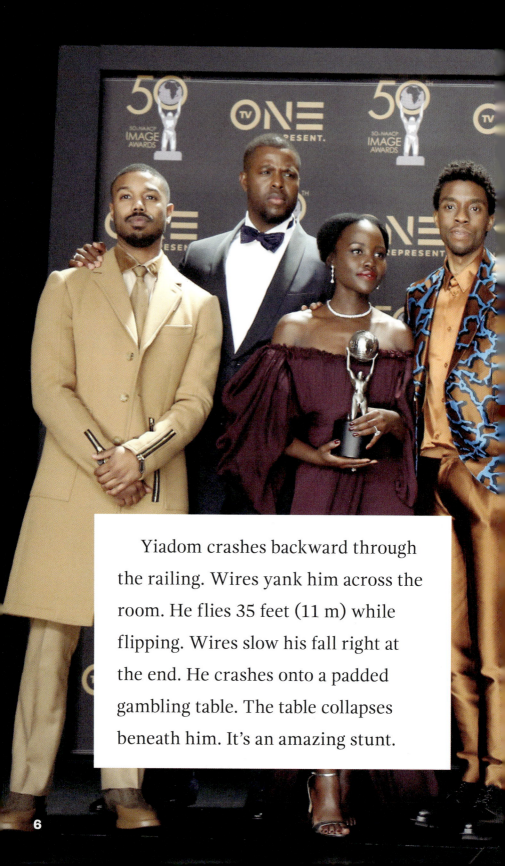

Yiadom crashes backward through the railing. Wires yank him across the room. He flies 35 feet (11 m) while flipping. Wires slow his fall right at the end. He crashes onto a padded gambling table. The table collapses beneath him. It's an amazing stunt.

The actors in *Black Panther* won many awards.

## LOTS OF STUNTS

*Black Panther* featured many stunts. They involved horses, car chases, and lots of fighting. More than 200 stunt performers worked on the movie. Many of the actors learned stunt skills, too. The stunt team won an award for their impressive work.

# Chapter 2
# KINDS OF STUNTS

**S**tunt performers do dangerous tricks. They may fall long distances, drive at high speeds, launch off jumps, or do other daring actions. These stunts are both risky and difficult.

For some stunts, people go flying off jumps on dirt bikes.

Some stunts involve huge leaps or falls. Performers climb up to high places. They may stand atop buildings or on cliffs. They may be hundreds of feet above the ground. Then, they leap through the air. Some land on another high-up place. Others plunge down toward the ground. Some use parachutes to slow their falls. Others land in nets or on airbags.

## HIGHEST FALL

In 1982, Dar Robinson did the highest fall stunt ever. He fell 1,100 feet (335 m) from a tall tower in Canada. He opened a parachute just seconds before he landed.

Dar Robinson jumped from the CN Tower in Toronto, Canada. He did this stunt for a movie.

Other stunts involve vehicles. Performers drive cars, motorcycles, boats, and more. They may race at high speeds. They may do sharp turns and tricky spins. Some performers do tricks in the air. They may fly off jumps. Or they may use airplanes or helicopters.

## SKY STUNTS

Some stunt performers skydive. They jump out of airplanes or helicopters. They fall thousands of feet. They do flips and spins on the way down.

An air show is an event where people do tricks that involve flying or skydiving.

13

Stunt performers may also work with fire. Some jump through fiery hoops. Others breathe fire or juggle burning objects. Some performers even light themselves on fire. All these performers wear fireproof clothes for protection. But the tricks are still dangerous. People can get badly burned.

In a fire dive, a performer jumps from a platform into a pool of water.

15

Other stunts involve fighting. Performers show off amazing kicks and punches. Many have training in martial arts. They leap, spin, and flip. They also learn ways to fall without getting hurt. These falls can be stunts, too. For instance, a person may tumble down a staircase or slam into a wall.

**Performers who throw knives practice hitting exactly the right spot.**

## WEAPON STUNTS

Some stunt performers use weapons. They may shoot arrows. Or they may throw knives at targets. Sometimes, they have people stand near the targets. But they aim very carefully so that no one gets hurt.

Chapter 3

# STUNTS ON SET

May stunt performers work on the sets of movies or TV shows. They help make action scenes look real. For example, they may use parkour to leap between the roofs of buildings.

People may use parkour moves while filming chase scenes.

Some stunt performers act as background characters in fight scenes. Others help with a single stunt. For instance, they may leap through a window. Or they may drive a car backward.

20

For some chase scenes, people attach cameras to cars. These cars drive to follow the action.

## DOUBLE DRIVING

Many movies have car-chase scenes. Stunt performers usually drive the vehicles. Some chase scenes have close-up shots. An actor sits inside the car and pretends to drive. But the car has a cage on its top. A stunt driver sits there and controls the car.

Stunt performers are often doubles. A double does stunts in place of a main actor in a movie or show. The double tries to look as much like this actor as possible. They wear the same clothes. They may use wigs and makeup, too. Cameras don't show the double's face. That makes it seem like the actor is doing the stunts.

## THEIR OWN STUNTS

Some actors do their own stunts. Bruce Lee often did this. His fighting skills helped make martial arts movies popular. Jackie Chan is another example. He began as a stunt performer. But he went on to star in many action movies.

Jackie Chan is best known for his martial arts skills. But he has done many types of stunts.

In some stunts, people do tricks on horseback.

Some people do many types of stunts. Others focus on certain types of tricks. For example, some performers work with animals. They may help with scenes where characters ride horses. They may have the horses jump. Or they may pretend to fight while riding.

## ACTION DOGS

In some movies and shows, dogs bite bad guys. Stunt performers help film these scenes. The dogs jump at the performers and bite them. The performers wear tough pads that the dogs can't bite through. Other people train the dogs. They help make sure everyone stays safe.

One fight scene often uses many performers and stunts. So, people must plan carefully. Stunt performers and actors work together. They practice each move. Most of the time, people just pretend to get hit or kicked. That way, they're less likely to get hurt.

During some scenes, performers wear wires. The wires can quickly pull people across a room. The people look like hits have sent them flying.

Wires help stunt performers leap or swing through the air.

27

**Chapter 4**

# LIVE STUNTS

Some people perform stunts in front of live audiences. Examples include circus acts and thrill shows. People come to watch performers show off their skills.

The WaterWorld thrill show is part of Universal Studios theme parks. It includes stunts done with boats.

At thrill shows, performers do daring tricks. The tricks often involve strength, speed, and balance. For example, some performers drive motorcycles. They may go flying off ramps. They may do spins and flips in the air. Some even jump through rings of fire.

## GLOBE OF DEATH

A globe of death is a large, round cage. Performers ride motorcycles inside it. They drive in circles and go upside down. Several performers may loop around the same cage at once. They must be very careful not to crash.

The motorcycles in a globe of death may go up to 65 miles per hour (105 km/h).

Circuses also include lots of stunts. Acrobats do many of them. These performers do tricks that involve balance and gymnastics. They may walk tightropes. They may hang from hoops or swings.

Often, acrobats have large nets below them. But sometimes, they have nothing to catch them if they fall.

## TEETERBOARDS

Some circuses use teeterboards. These look like long planks. A performer stands at one end. Another person jumps onto the other end. This launches the first person high into the air. That person does flips or tricks. Then they land and launch the other person.

**Tightrope walkers often carry long poles to help with balance.**

Some performers do shows alone. Other times, performers work in teams. For example, some thrill shows feature tricks done on water. Boats pull people on water skis. These people sometimes form stacks. They climb up onto one another's backs or shoulders. In circuses, acrobats may perform in groups. They toss and catch one another while swinging from hoops or bars.

Acrobats who use swinging bars to do tricks are called trapeze artists.

Performers work to wow audiences. Many stunts are extremely difficult. Some seem impossible. For example, performers may swallow swords. Others swallow fire. They may breathe fire, too. These tricks take lots of time and practice to learn.

**A few fire-breathers can shoot flames 15 feet (4.6 m) or more.**

# FIRE-BREATHING

A fire-breather holds a torch in front of their face. They hold some kind of fuel in their mouth. Then, they blow the fuel at the torch. Huge flames shoot out. The person takes care so they don't swallow the fuel or get burned.

## Story Spotlight

# EVEL KNIEVEL

Evel Knievel was a famous daredevil. He began performing motorcycle stunts in the 1960s. He rode off huge ramps and jumped over dozens of cars and vans.

One of his most famous stunts took place in 1967. Knievel tried to jump over fountains at a hotel in Las Vegas, Nevada. He flew 141 feet (43 m). But he landed poorly. He fell off the motorcycle and hit his head. He was in a coma for a month. But he survived.

**Evel Knievel set many stunt records, including the record for most broken bones.**

# Chapter 5
# BIG RISKS

Doing stunts is always risky. People plan and practice. But if something goes wrong, they can get badly hurt. People can break many bones. They can also get serious burns or become paralyzed. They may even die.

For one movie stunt, filmmakers blew up a bus in London, England.

On sets, people work to limit the risks of stunts. They may use fake weapons in fight scenes. For example, they may use swords with edges that are dull and rounded. Or they may have guns shoot blanks instead of bullets. But mistakes still happen. People can get hurt or killed.

## BUSTER KEATON

Buster Keaton became a film stuntman in the early 1900s. He appeared in more than 100 movies and shows. During his career, he broke almost every bone in his body. During one stunt, he broke his neck. Amazingly, he kept right on filming.

People fire guns for a scene in the Netflix film *The Gray Man*.

43

Safety equipment helps limit some risks. For example, stunt drivers can wear helmets or neck braces. Harnesses help, too. Their straps keep drivers from flying out of vehicles. But bad crashes can still happen. Drivers can get hurt or killed.

Safety equipment sometimes fails, too. Wires may not catch people like they are supposed to. Harnesses may break. Performers can get badly hurt. Some injuries are permanent.

A plane crashed to the ground during a stunt show in Ohio in 2013. Two people died.

**Many stunts involve falls or crashes, even if done correctly.**

Even stunts that go as planned can cause problems. During fights or falls, performers may take hits or slam onto pads. Small injuries can build up over time. This can be hard on people's bodies.

## HEAD INJURIES

If stunt performers get hit in the head, they can get concussions. Concussions are injuries to the brain. They can cause pain or throwing up. They can also make it hard for people to think, see, or remember things.

# Story Spotlight

# DAVID HOLMES

David Holmes was a stunt double for the Harry Potter film series. He did stunts for Daniel Radcliffe. But in 2009, Holmes got hurt. He was filming a scene for *Harry Potter and the Deathly Hallows: Part 1.*

In the scene, Harry Potter fights a snake. Holmes was on wires. That way, he could fly back quickly after a hit. But the wires pulled him too fast. He hit the mats too hard and broke his neck. He became paralyzed.

**After a stunt went wrong, David Holmes needed to use a wheelchair.**

Performers who juggle knives or torches can get badly hurt if they grab the wrong end.

# Chapter 6

# TYPES OF TRAINING

Because their work is so dangerous, stunt performers must spend many hours training and practicing. Their aim and timing must be exactly right.

Many people start by going to stunt school. Courses there cover different skills. Some courses last a few weeks. They teach basic skills in many areas. Students learn how to do falls from high places or in fights. They practice fighting and using weapons for scenes. Some courses also cover wire stunts and driving.

Some stunt drivers can tilt a car on just two wheels.

53

Some performers choose to specialize. They get extra training in certain skills. For instance, they may focus on flying planes. Or they may learn to do stunts underwater. Stunt performers may take acting lessons as well. That can help them make the scenes they are in feel real.

## FIRE STUNTS

Performers who work with fire learn extra safety tips. They learn ways to keep fire from spreading. And they keep water or fire extinguishers nearby. For some tricks, performers practice without fire. For example, a juggler might use torches. They toss just the torches first. They add the fire later.

For some stunts, pilots fly very close to other planes.

Many stunts require lots of strength. So, stunt performers must build muscle. They spend lots of time working out. They run, climb, lift weights, and more.

Often, stunt performers have long workdays. They may need to do stunts for many hours. If performers get worn out, they are more likely to get hurt. So, performers train to build endurance. This helps them keep being careful and precise.

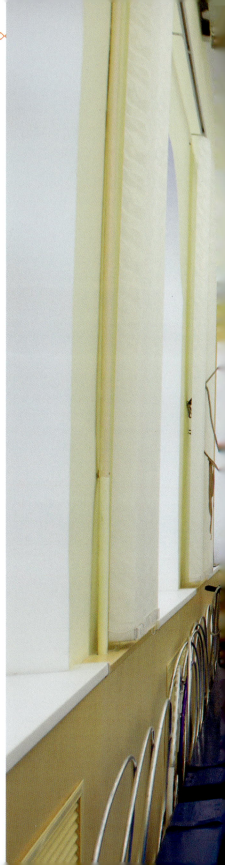

Some kids attend circus schools. They start learning stunts at a young age.

## STUNT SKILLS

Some stunt performers use skills they bring from other areas of life. For example, some started as dancers. Others played sports or did gymnastics. People may also become stunt drivers after working as police officers.

# ✓ SKILLS CHECKLIST

- Able to perform well under pressure

- Good at working with others

- Maintains excellent physical fitness

- Pays careful attention to safety rules

- Has experience with stunt driving

- Trained in martial arts

# COMPREHENSION QUESTIONS

*Write your answers on a separate piece of paper.*

1. Write a paragraph that explains the main ideas in Chapter 3.

2. Would you want to be a stunt performer? Why or why not?

3. What does an acrobat do?
   A. tricks that copy an actor
   B. tricks that involve balance
   C. tricks that involve car chases

4. What could happen if stunt performers didn't work out?
   A. They could get better at acting.
   B. They could stop being strong enough to do stunts.
   C. They could do all their stunts perfectly.

**5.** What does **plunge** mean in this book?

*Others **plunge** down toward the ground. Some use parachutes to slow their falls. Others land in nets or on airbags.*

    **A.** climb slowly

    **B.** drop quickly

    **C.** take classes

**6.** What does **tough** mean in this book?

*The dogs jump at the performers and bite them. The performers wear **tough** pads that the dogs can't bite through.*

    **A.** thick and strong

    **B.** thin and weak

    **C.** just pretend

*Answer key on page 64.*

# GLOSSARY

**blanks**
Shell casings that have gunpowder but no bullets.

**casino**
A place where people play games to try to win money.

**coma**
A state of being unconscious, often as a result of being sick or hurt.

**daredevil**
A person who does risky things, often for show.

**endurance**
The ability to keep doing something for a long time.

**equipment**
Tools or machines used to do a job.

**fire extinguishers**
Tools that shoot water, foam, or gas to put out fires.

**gymnastics**
A sport where people do tricks using mats, rings, bars, or beams.

**parachutes**
Fabric that opens to slow people as they fall through the air.

**paralyzed**
Not able to move part of the body.

**parkour**
The skill of running, climbing, and jumping to move quickly through an area.

# TO LEARN MORE

## BOOKS

James, Thomas. *BMX Champ: Acrobats on a Bike.* Knowledge Books, 2024.

Loh-Hagan, Virginia. *Weird Science: Movies.* Cherry Lake Publishing, 2022.

Stevenson, Paul. *Stunt Performers on Film.* Hungry Tomato, 2025.

## ONLINE RESOURCES

Visit **www.apexeditions.com** to find links and resources related to this title.

## ABOUT THE AUTHOR

Abby Doty is a writer, editor, and booklover from Minnesota.

# INDEX

action, 8, 18, 22, 25
actors, 4, 7, 21–22, 26
airplanes, 12, 54
animals, 25
audiences, 28, 36
award, 7

car chases, 7, 21
circus, 28, 32, 34

fighting, 7, 16, 20, 22, 25–26, 42, 47, 48, 52
fire, 14, 30, 36–37, 54

helmets, 44
hurt, 16–17, 26, 40, 42, 44, 48, 56

injuries, 44, 47

jumping, 12, 14, 25, 30, 32, 38
jumps, 8, 12

parachutes, 10
practice, 26, 36, 40, 51–52, 54
protection, 14

safety, 44, 54
scenes, 18, 20–21, 25–26, 42, 48, 52, 54
skills, 7, 22, 28, 52, 54, 57

teams, 7, 34
thrill shows, 28, 30, 34
training, 16, 25, 51, 54, 56
TV shows, 18, 22, 25, 42

vehicles, 12, 21, 44

weapons, 17, 42, 52
wires, 6, 26, 44, 48, 52

## ANSWER KEY:

1. Answers will vary; 2. Answers will vary; 3. B; 4. B; 5. B; 6. A